Michael Daugherty

Raise the Roof
(for Timpani and Orchestra)

(2003)

Solo Timpani Part

HENDON MUSIC

BOOSEY &HAWKES

DISTRIBUTED BY

HAL•LEONARD®
CORPORATION
7777 W. BLUEMOUND RD. P.O. BOX 13819 MILWAUKEE, WI 53213

www.boosey.com
www.halleonard.com

RAISE THE ROOF
for Timpani and Orchestra

MICHAEL DAUGHERTY
(2003)

TIMPANI

Rev. 15 Apr. 2009

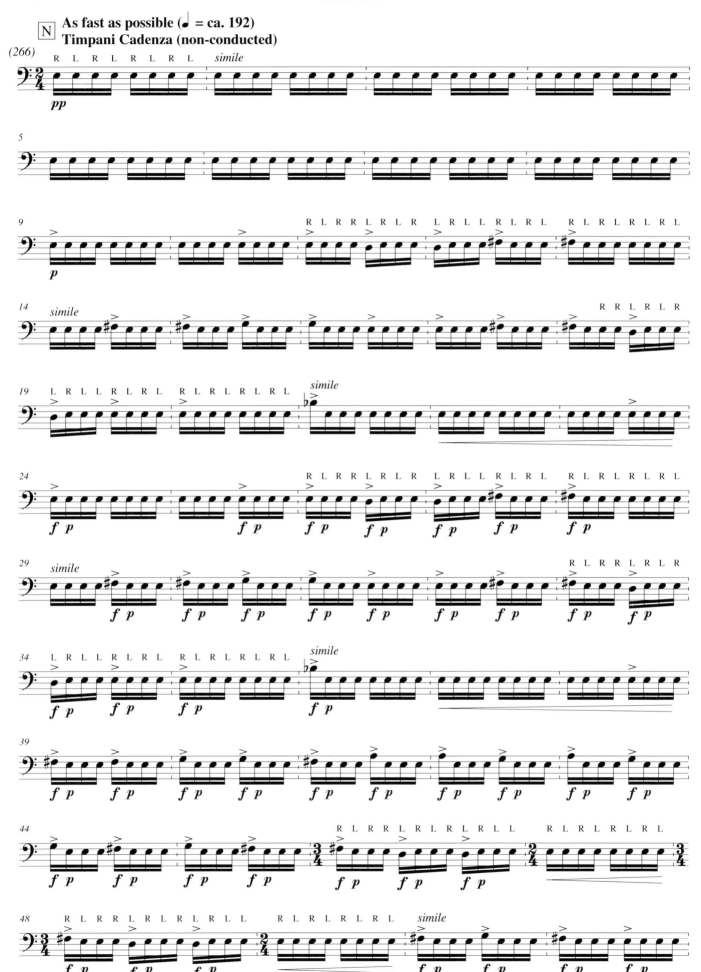

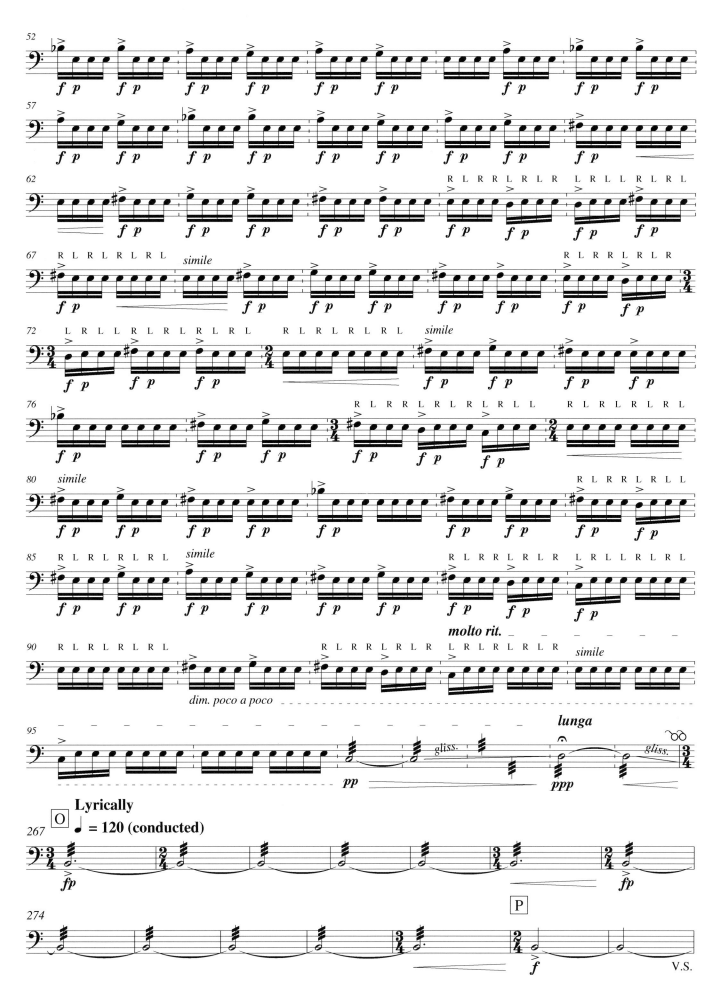

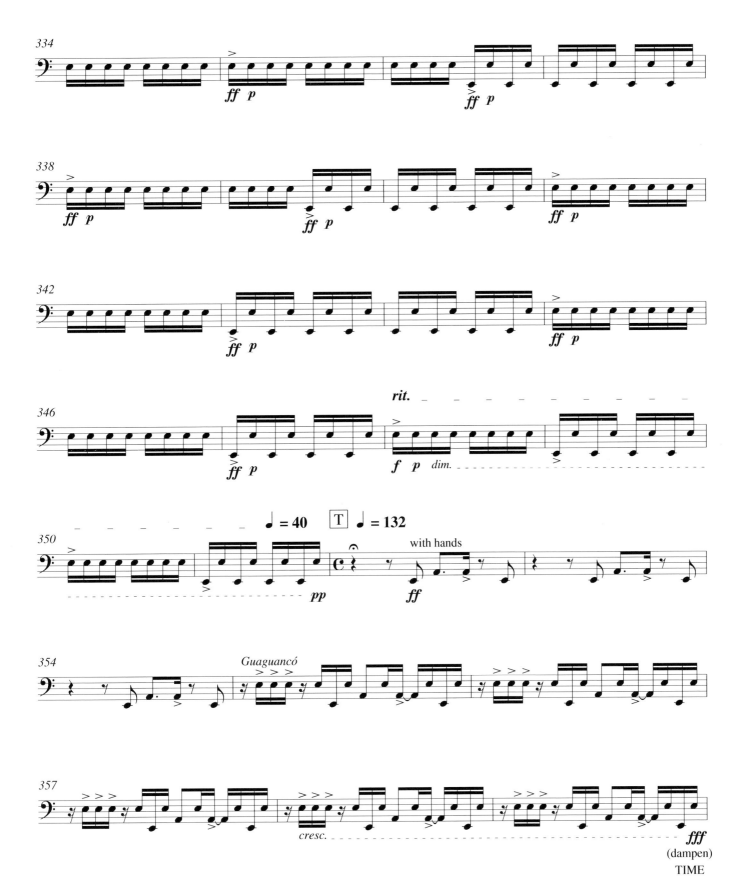

U

360 dampen

V

372 Wire brushes

375

378

381

V.S.